IMAGES OF WALES

AROUND
CRICKHOWELL

CROSS STREET

SUGAR LOAF MOUNTAIN

ABERGAVENNY

VALE OF LLANTHONY

USK BRIDGE

IMAGES OF WALES

AROUND
CRICKHOWELL

DAVID EDGE AND NICHOLAS SEABOURNE

TEMPUS

Frontispiece: A 1960s postcard view of Abergavenny, showing Cross Street, the Vale of Llanthony, the Sugar Loaf and Usk road bridge.

First published 2005

Tempus Publishing Limited
The Mill, Brimscombe Port,
Stroud, Gloucestershire, GL5 2QG
www.tempus-publishing.com

British Library Cataloguing in Publication Data.
A catalogue record for this book is available from the British Library.

ISBN 0 7524 3638 4

Typesetting and origination by Tempus Publishing Limited.
Printed in Great Britain.

Contents

Acknowledgements

We would like to thank everyone who helped in compiling this book. These are R.M. Casserley, Les Knight, Nigel Lewis, Kathleen and Jim Parker, Betty and Larry Thomas and Howard Williams.

The omission of any names or infringements of any copyright are entirely unintentional.

Introduction

I came to live in Gilwern in 1961 with my parents Sheila and Robert Edge and my younger sister Siân. Gilwern was a far smaller village than it is today and did not have a doctor's surgery. As a result, we joined the practice of Herdman, Humphries and Morgan in the small market town of Crickhowell. In order to visit the doctor, I was taken by Red and White bus to Crickhowell as my father could not drive at the time. More often than not, my mother would take me but on some occasions my father would take me. Often he would decide to walk back home carrying me on his shoulder. We would sometimes visit Crickhowell Castle or walk past Cwrt Y Gollen army camp, where we would see various army vehicles, or the soldiers training. My father, like many men of his generation, had been required to do National Service and had served with the British Army between 1955 and 1958; passing the camp reminded him of his days as a soldier. Later, after a serious accident in which I stepped into a bag of lime, I was for a number of years required to visit Crickhowell Hospital for treatment. Thus during the first ten years of my life I visited Crickhowell frequently and over the years have seen the many changes to the town that have taken place.

As I grew up, I became interested in history and often visited castles, such as that at Abergavenny, with my parents. While my first interest is railways, especially South Wales railways, my interest in history, including local history, has encouraged me to write books and articles on these subjects. During the twenty-three years that I spent living in first Gilwern and later Clydach, I learnt a lot regarding the past in this area. *Around Crickhowell* is a follow-up to *Around Gilwern* and I have attempted to give the reader an insight into the past of the area, for example it is not commonly known that the world's largest mountain was named after George Everest, who came from the town of Crickhowell, and who at one time had been India's Surveyor General. The book is not an in-depth history but I hope it will be informative and enjoyable to all who read it.

I would also like to record a very special thanks to my very dear friend Carol Hopkins, without whose help, support, encouragement and loyalty during a very difficult time this book would not have been completed.

David Edge
April 2005

About the Authors

David Edge was born in London in 1958 and moved to Gilwern in 1961. Educated first at Gilwern Primary School and then Brynmawr Comprehensive School, he started work in 1974. His first job was that of Sales Assistant at Hodge's Menswear in Abergavenny, later transferring to the Brecon branch. Between 1977 and 1985 he worked at ROF Glascoed before taking up a position with a security company in London. During the 1980s and early 1990s he worked on the railway for Network South East in the Reading area, reaching the position of School Safety Adviser. He is now employed by the MOD, working in the Gloucester area.

During his younger days he represented both Gilwern Harriers and Brynmawr Comprehensive School at both cross-country and track events; he also represented the school at rugby. Playing football for a number of years, he represented Gilwern Cubs and Scouts and played for Clydach, Llanfoist and Pandy at senior level. He has had a lifelong interest in railways and local history. Previous publications include *Around Gilwern* and *Hereford United* and he is frequently asked to give talks to societies and clubs.

Nicholas Seabourne was born in Gilwern in 1958, the only child of Gwyn and Barbara Seabourne. Educated at Gilwern Primary School and Brynmawr Comprehensive School, he completed his teacher training at Swansea University. A keen member of Gilwern Harriers, he is well known in the district for his running. He has a lifelong interest in Welsh history, which includes canals, railways and tram roads. Over the years he has collected a vast number of photographs and postcards of the bygone days of the area and many are included in this publication. He first met David Edge at Gilwern Primary School and the two have remained lifelong friends. Following the career of his mother, who for many years taught at Govilon School, he now teaches Welsh at schools and colleges. He has on occasions been asked to translate old documents from Welsh to English and regularly attends the Evangelical church at Crickhowell.

one

Crickhowell

Crickhowell (from the fields.)

The picturesque town of Crickhowell from the Llangattock side, looking across the River Usk. The bridge is known locally as the Town Bridge. Crickhowell stands on rising ground on the left bank of the River Usk, about 14 miles south-east from Brecon. Referred to in Welsh as Crug Hywei (Hywel's Cairn), it is today a very popular tourist attraction. The town is 300ft above sea level and continues to expand in population. Nearby is the Breannog mountain, part of the Black Mountains, which shelters the vale from the north winds. The bold and rugged Darren mountain overlooks the village of Llangattock, which lies just opposite Crickhowell on the other side of the river. A weekly market is held in Crickhowell; it dates from medieval times when the people from the hills came down and carried away much of the farm produce of the vale.

Above and below: Two views of Crickhowell from the Llangattock side. The town has an interesting history: it is perhaps not widely known that before the Union of England and Wales in 1535, Crickhowell was distinct from the county of Brecknock. At that time, it was under the rule of the Lords Marcher, its governor being the Lord of Blaenllyfni Castle. Things changed during the reign of Henry VIII, when the town became part of the county and was made the principal town of the Crickhowell hundred. The manor of Crickhowell was given to Sir Humphrey de Burghill during the reign of King William II and later passed into the hands of the Turbervilles.

This fourteen-arch bridge spans the River Usk. Trout and salmon swim in the river and the district is popular with anglers. The bridge dates from the seventeenth century and is the subject of myth, the reason being that it is possible to see thirteen arches from the eastern end while only twelve are visible from the west.

St Edmund's church and Table Mountain are visible in this view of the town, seen from the Llangattock side. Several handsome houses make the town one of the most picturesque to be found in Breconshire. It is probable that the town was first built in around AD 940, during the reign of Hywel Dda, Prince of South Wales.

A young man fishing on the bank of the River Usk at Crickhowell with a rod made from a tree branch. The peace and tranquillity make the river popular with anglers. Arguably, the most sporting and difficult angling method is fly-fishing, widely used for catching trout. The fly angler uses a rod much longer – up to 3m (10ft) – and lighter than rods used for bait- and spin-fishing. To cast such a small offering, the angler whips the fly rod back and forth until a considerable amount of line is in the air. Casts are made to likely looking spots, such as pools and pockets in streams, where the fly is allowed to touch the water and then float (dry fly-fishing) or sink (wet fly-fishing). If a fish strikes, the angler pulls in line while raising the rod tip to set the hook in the fish's mouth. The angler fights the fish by pulling in the line by hand or by reeling line onto the reel.

An advertisement for the Bridge End Hotel, Crickhowell, which at that time was owned by Mr and Mrs Jack Townsend. The hotel, located near to the Town Bridge, was once an old tollhouse and has withstood the damage caused by the river bursting its banks on many occasions. ‘

A show in progress at the Agricultural Show Field in Crickhowell. There is no doubt that the improvements in transportation affected agriculture: roads, canals and railways enabled farmers to obtain needed supplies and to market their produce over a much wider area. Food could be protected in transport and shipped more economically than before as a result of the rail, ship and refrigeration developments of the late nineteenth and early twentieth centuries. The agricultural show has always been a blessing to not only the farmers of Breconshire but also the landowners and local businessmen. The farmer's wife was able to sell her products, such as cheese and cakes, and a fun day could be had by all. Livestock could be exhibited and sold, bartering took place and healthy outdoor pursuits such as tug-of-war competitions were held.

Opposite page: Two views of the Crickhowell Harriers setting off on a hunt. Hunting, often referred to as the sport of kings, was at one time designed for the pursuing and killing of wild game animals in order to provide food. People have been hunting since prehistoric times to provide themselves and their families with food, fur and leather clothing, and hides for shelter. With the development of agriculture, animal husbandry and, eventually, manufacturing, hunting gradually diminished in importance as a means of survival and became a sport simply for the thrill of the chase or for the enjoyment of outdoor life. The horses and hounds at meetings such as Boxing Day was considered by many to be a magnificent sight.

CRICKHOWELL HARRIERS

The main street in Crickhowell, *c.* 1925. Crickhowell was one of the main market towns of the county, the space in this street being ideal for the setting up of stalls. The Bear Hotel can be seen on the left of the drinking fountain in the centre. The fountain was the gift of the late Sir Joseph Bailey, Lord Glanusk. It has been said that the town had at one time consisted of one street, reaching down to the bridge over the Usk; nowadays this is not the case. The county town of Brecon is approximately 13 miles away from Crickhowell, while London is approximately 151 miles away.

The main street in around 1910. The Town Hall, on the left, was built at the expense of the Duke of Beaufort. The ground floor was used as a market-place, while the first floor served at one time for the business of the police and county courts. At one time, the town was well known for its flannel manufacture but besides a few factories in the neighbourhood, there is now sadly nothing remaining.

A Great Western Railway bus awaits passengers in Crickhowell, *c.* 1910. There had once been plans to build a railway from Abergavenny to Brecon via Crickhowell but this project was scrapped. Thus the Great Western Railway decided to try their own bus service, which met with some success for a time.

The local YMCA in Crickhowell, *c.* 1920. The YMCA was founded in London in 1844 in response to unhealthy social conditions arising in large cities at the end of the Industrial Revolution, as a result of which many young men from rural areas came to work in the cities. Far from home and family, after work these youths were often drawn into gambling houses and other disreputable establishments. In 1844 the British humanitarian Sir George Williams organised the first Young Men's Christian Association, which attempted to combat idleness among young workers by means of Bible studies and prayer meetings. The YMCA idea proved very popular and by 1851 Great Britain had 2,700 members in twenty-four associations. Today this worldwide organisation serves communities all over the world.

Above and below: Porthmawr Gateway, Crickhowell. This historic gateway has stood the test of time and is arguably one of the finest and most impressive stone gatehouses in the county.

This view of Crickhowell in around 1920 clearly shows the way in which the town climbs the hillside away from the River Usk. The town has been known to flood on many occasions.

The ruins of Crickhowell Castle are just visible on the left of this picture, which dates from around 1920. The castle was one of the thirteen Norman castles erected in the county. It stands on the western side of the town, on the left of the road leading from Abergavenny. The present ruins are only a small portion of the old castle, which occupied a space of eight acres. The castle tump commands a fine view of the landscape and is the site of the keep, a lofty square building, four storeys high, whose vaults are no doubt beneath the present ruins. Houses have now been built on the site of the castle. Ivy Tower, a house standing in Standard Street, was once part of the old fortress site.

Crickhowell has a rich history. In 1172 the castle of Crickhowell was stormed and its garrison taken prisoners by a Monmouthshire chieftain; it was later regained for the King. During the reign of Edward I, Sir Hugh de Turberville was in charge of the castle and he raised troops in Wales for the King's service. Other Norman nobles commanded the castle at various times, including Sir Grimbald de Pauncefote, who obtained permission from Henry III to hold a weekly market and an annual fair in the town on 12 May. In 1403 Henry IV gave orders to Sir John, son of Sir Grimbald, to fortify and defend his castle against the attacks of the most famous of the Welsh Princes, Owain Glyndwr. The defences failed and, as time went by, Glyndwr succeeded in destroying not only Crickhowell Castle but also many others in the county. The manor of Crickhowell was under the rule of the Lord of Blaenllyfni and Dinas, near LIangorse, but Edward IV granted the manors of Crickhowell and Tretower to his friend and favourite Sir William Herbert of Raglan Castle, whom he later created Earl of Pembroke. His daughter, Lady Elizabeth Herbert, conveyed these estates by marriage to Sir Charles Somerset, from whom they have descended into the hands of the present owner, the Duke of Beaufort.

New Road, Crickhowell. This small market town has changed over the years but without, in many cases, redevelopment taking place. In around 1800 the Brecon, Carmarthen and Milford stagecoach would pass through the town twice a week and wagons loaded with goods would also pass through en route to London and Bristol. Today, buses and lorries pass through the town, often carrying out the same duties. The town has slowly expanded and the area now has more housing, a better school and is in reality a dormitory town for nearby cities, because the modern roads make the distances easy to travel. One of the main industries in the town today is tourism and many visitors from all over the world enjoy their time visiting the charming and interesting town.

Glanusk Park, Crickhowell. Joseph Russell Bailey, afterwards Lord Glanusk, was born in Leamington on 7 April 1840 and his early days were spent at Penymarth, near Crickhowell. He was related to ironmaster Crawshay Bailey. After completing his education at Harrow and Oxford, he spent some time touring the Continent. He married Mary Anne, daughter of Henry Lucas MD of Glanyrafon, Crickhowell and the stately mansion of Glanusk, was their home. Sir Joseph was born 'with a silver spoon in his mouth', inheriting great wealth and succeeding to the title of Baronet on his grandfather's death. Sir Joseph was endowed with a commercial aptitude, immense business ability and a strong and ready brain, a steady purpose, and tireless energy. His father had died when he was ten years old and this would appear to have a sobering effect on his character, an influence that seemed to remain throughout his life. Sir Joseph decided early in life to give his leisure time to serve his fellow men. He was made JP and at the age of twenty-four the Queen appointed him High Sheriff of Breconshire. For many years he was chairman of the Crickhowell Board of Guardians and of various other public bodies. In 1865 he became MP for Herefordshire, a position which he filled with dignity for twenty years.

Sir Joseph was a keen antiquarian and archaeologist. He earned the affection and esteem of his tenants because their welfare was one of his chief considerations. Duty was his watchword and he generously gave it to the service of the community. In thanksgiving for the recovery of one his children from a dangerous attack of scarlet fever, Sir Joseph restored St John's church, Tretower. He built the Parish Room connected with it to commemorate his silver wedding. When Lord Tredegar, Lord Lieutenant of the County, died in 1875, Sir Joseph succeeded him and for thirty years he carried out his duties of office. In 1888 he was elected County Councillor for the Llangattock division, being unopposed for the remainder of his time in office. When the National Eisteddfod visited Brecon in 1889, he acted as president, taking the place of the Prince of Wales.

Sir Joseph retired from Parliament in 1892 and was later honoured with a peerage. He was chairman of Breconshire County Council for many years. He passed away in January 1906.

The magnificent spectacle and rugged beauty of the Brecon Beacons, which look down upon the Wye from a height of nearly 3,000ft. On their eastern side, the lakes run from Vaynor and the Taf Fechan reservoir to Tal-y-bont and Llangorse lake. To the west, the Fan hills of the Fforest Fawr carry the Roman road, the *Sarn Helen*, that supplied the forts set above the Wye. From Pen Milan it is possible to see the Black Mountains as they tower above Hay-on-Wye and the Mynydd Epynt that rises over Builth Wells. The Beacons also look southward to Aberdare, Mountain Ash, and Merthyr Tydfil. The flooding of the valley to make the Taf Fechan reservoir changed the character of the area forever. The remote area was until December 1962 served by the Brecon to Newport railway, which had a small halt for Dol-y-gaer (meaning 'meadow where the Roman fort was'), where there was a fifteenth-century church and a community of people. The closure of the line came around forty years after the valley was drowned.

Visitors to the Brecon Beacons will agree that nowhere can there exist a more graceful group of heights, and it can be argued that their form is equal to, if not grander than, the perhaps more famous heights in the Lake District of England and in North Wales. Whatever the reason for tourists to be in the area, they cannot fail to have seen the awe-inspiring beauty, ruggedness and the hostile hidden danger of the countryside. To anyone left alone or unprepared for the inclement weather, the Brecon Beacons can bring disaster in a relatively short time. The Beacons are the highest mountains in South Wales. The view from the top is rewarding for those brave enough to make the climb. On a clear day it is quite possible to see the Bristol Channel. The military forces of Great Britain are among the many who use the beacons for training exercises. It is not unusual for the emergency services to be scrambled to locate missing climbers, walkers or service personnel. The beauty of this remote range attracts all who visit the area.

Llynsafaddan, or Llangorse Lake, near Brecon is a very popular tourist attraction today and has been for well over 100 years. It is arguably one of the most interesting of all the prehistoric remains in the county; Revd E.N. Dumbleton MA is known to have explored the lake around 1867. On the north end of the lake is a small island, nearly square in shape and about 90 yards in circumference, which was at one time a lake dwelling made by some of the early inhabitants of the country. A site on the lake was chosen for the sake of safety from wild animals and robbers that might attack them. The lake is the largest sheet of water in South Wales and lies in a hollow about 6 miles south-east of the town of Brecon. The country around is exceedingly pleasing and pretty. On the east of the lake, the hills of Llangorse rise, with the peak called Mynydd Troed forming the north end. Beyond are the Black Mountains and the picturesque country around Talgarth.

Like many ancient places in Wales, Llangorse Lake is steeped in history, myth and legend. Rumours of the sunken city, perhaps *Loventium*, lying beneath the lake have always been with us. 'The Old Woman of Llangorse will grip you' was a threat that parents hurled at disobedient children who went in a boat on the lake. The old woman was said to sit upon the vane of the steeple of the buried church and in a pitiful voice invite the child to her; the child would then disappear with the old mother forever beneath its waters. Another legend says that the spot now covered by the lake was once a beautiful valley, with the Llyfni flowing through to join the Wye. On its left bank stood the church of Llangasty and on the other side stood the fortified palace of a prince who feared not God nor respected man and who scorned religion and hated everything beautiful and good. And so the legends go on.

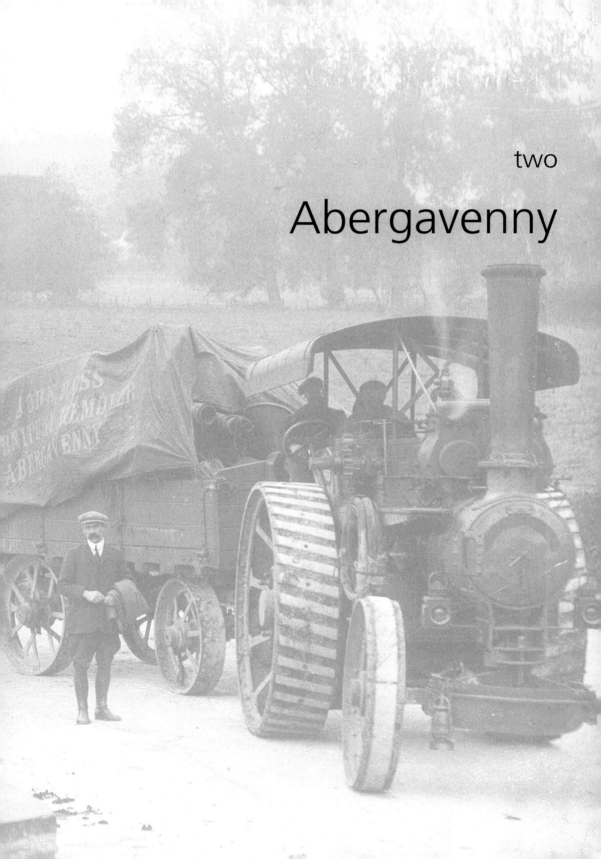

two

Abergavenny

ABERGAVENNY CASTLE.

FROM MONMOUTH ROAD.

WAR MEMORIAL
ABERGAVENNY

ABERGAVENNY &
HOLY MOUNTAIN.

CROSS STREET. (1)

Abergavenny, c. 1920. The ancient market town of Abergavenny, close to the border with England, has an interesting history. A settlement is known to have existed here since Roman times. This was the beginning of the rich but sometimes violent history of the town, which includes events ranging from the massacre by William de Braose at Abergavenny Castle in 1177 to the visit of The Beatles to the town in June 1963. Sporting achievements include Sir Harry Llewelyn and his horse Foxhunter, who in the 1952 Olympics in Helsinki helped win a gold medal for Great Britain. In football circles, Abergavenny Thursdays, originally formed by the town's shopkeepers, have a certain standing in Welsh football. Their successes include winning the Welsh League Challenge Cup in 1952 and 1959.

Opposite above: Standing sentinel around the town of Abergavenny are four noble hills. The graceful cone of the Sugar Loaf stands to the north. Its height of just under 2,000ft distinguishes it from the main mass of the Black Mountains and it covers an area of around 2,130 acres. The mountain was given to the National Trust as a memorial to Lord Rhondda.

Opposite below: To the east of Abergavenny is Ysgyryd Fach, or Little Skirrid, which stands at 886ft. Across the Usk rises the massive Blorenge, at 1,834ft, a mountain of old red sandstone capped with limestone cliffs. To the north-east is Ysgyryd Fawr, or the Skirrid, at 1,596ft; here another 205 acres belong to the National Trust. The town of Abergavenny can be found nestling in the centre of this ring of hills.

The Usk and Little Skirrid, Abergavenny

With its favoured position at the point where the River Usk leaves the mountains, the market town of Abergavenny has always been a strong base for anyone trying to invade South Wales. The Romans seem to have had a fort here, *Gobannium*, but the town enters fully into history with the arrival of the Normans. William Rufus gave Abergavenny to Hamelin de Balun. Later it became the stronghold of the famous Marcher family of De Braose. It was a William de Braose, one of the most notable of the clan, who made Abergavenny a place hated for 200 years in the eyes of the Welsh. This powerful baron, who combined unctuous piety with ruthlessness in a way peculiar to the Normans, succeeded to his inheritance in 1177.

William de Braose signalled his entrance into history by inviting Seissyll, the most important of the neighbouring Welsh rulers, together with numerous other prominent Welshmen from Gwent, to a banquet in the castle. He had them mercilessly put to death as they feasted. Not content with this, he sent his retainers post haste to Seissyll's castle. Here they seized his wife and killed his young son, Cadwaladr, in his mother's arms. The Welsh took revenge by capturing Abergavenny Castle but William de Braose, in the way of the wicked, flourished for thirty years, until he met his match in King John. John stripped him of his lands and left him to die a beggar.

Above and below: Abergavenny in the county of Monmouthshire is proud of its title, the Gateway to Wales, and the town is located in a wonderful setting. The River Usk passes the town and then swings southwards towards the distant sea. Not even the progress of new buildings around the town, together with redevelopment of the site where Cooper's Filters (once the town's largest employer) stood, can mar this fine composition of mountain and river scenery. The town itself may not be remarkable architecturally but it has the life and bustle of a country market centre and contains some ancient monuments that make it worthy of its setting. The town has continued to expand since the 1960s and the Tuesday market is still a popular attraction to both locals and visitors.

The Castle and Little Skirrid, Abergavenny from River.

Cross Street, Abergavenny.

St Mary's church is considered by many to be the greatest glory of Abergavenny. It was originally the church of the Benedictine priory founded by Hamelin de Balun. The Benedictines were the favoured monks of the Norman Marcher barons, as the Carthusians were of the Welsh, and the priory grew under the protective shadow of the castle. It was ransacked by Owain Glyndwr's men when they set fire to the town during the wild Glyndwr Revolt. Little now remains of the priory buildings although some of the walls run alongside the little River Gavenny, from which the town gets its name. Two noble trees, a chestnut and a sycamore, give shade to the site. Henry VIII dissolved the priory in 1543 and used the income to found the grammar school. He converted the priory church into the town church of St Mary. The grammar school, which was used during the Second World War to house American troops, was demolished during the 1950s.

Opposite above: The now ruined Abergavenny Castle stands as a monument to its violent history, on the wooded hill where it once dominated the town. Still visible today are the gatehouse, some walls, the motte and the foundations of the keep. The castle came into the possession of the Nevill family in the fifteenth century.

Opposite below: The barony of Abergavenny was not created but is attached to the possession of the castle. Cross Street, *c.* 1910. On the left is the Angel Hotel. The Town Hall, which was built in the nineteenth century, can be seen in the centre. Arguably a Gothic triumph of red stone with a green-topped tower, it has a large clock, which was presented by the ironmaster Crawshay Bailey.

Today, Abergavenny is perhaps not considered to be a stronghold of Welsh speakers but in the nineteenth century the efforts of Sir Benjamin Hall and his wife, later Lord and Lady Llanover, made the town an important centre in the movement to revive Welsh culture. As a result of their efforts, the literary society of Cymreigyddion y Fenni was inaugurated and for nearly thirty years the annual Eisteddfodau drew all that was best in the world of Wales to Abergavenny. Sadly, with the death of Lord Llanover came the end of the Eisteddfod. Once again Abergavenny returned to its natural vocation, which was that of a pleasant, busy market town.

Abergavenny is the starting-point of the Heads of the Valleys road that runs from the outskirts of the town, up through the Clydach vale under the Blorenge mountain and so on to the tops of the mining valleys that are located in this region. The Usk valley and the Black Mountains, together with the Brecon Beacons, are now all part of the Brecon Beacons National Park. Abergavenny is considered to be the natural gateway to the park.

An undated picture of the town of Abergavenny, in the valley of the River Usk. A visitor to this location today would notice the considerable amount of changes that have occurred over the last century.

High Street, Abergavenny, *c.* 1910. The shop on the left became Hodge's Menswear in 1969, under the managership of Mr Ken Shepherd. Many local men worked at the store until its closure in 1998, including Mr Ken Prosser, Mr Lyndon Prosser and Mr Gary Thatcher.

Frogmore Street, Abergavenny, *c.* 1910. Once known as the West End to local inhabitants, this was at one time considered to be the upmarket area of the town.

Abergavenny has buildings that date from the Tudor period onwards, and they all seem to fit into place. As with many towns, the level of the road has risen continuously through the centuries and it is possible, by searching at ground level, to spot the occasional Tudor archways and windows that survive. The old tower, with its battlements, belonged to the former parish church of St John. Beside it is the Masonic Hall, built on the site of the old grammar school. Among the churches of the town is the Roman Catholic church built opposite the grammar school at Pen-y-Pound.

A view of the Sugar Loaf mountain, *c.* 1950. The freight train in the foreground reminds us of the days when steam was king and most freight was transported by rail.

This traction engine and trailers belonged to the John Ross furniture removal company of Abergavenny. The company was still trading in 1922, when the business of coal and timber merchants was added to their impressive portfolio, but sadly the company no longer exists. Traction engines were a common sight

on the roads of Great Britain for many years. The photograph is believed to have been taken around 1910 in Bailey Park, which is perhaps a fitting location as the Abergavenny Steam Show, with its many traction engines, is held here and attracts many visitors each year.

Llanfihangel Court, near Abergavenny. This fine mansion displays all the grandeur of bygone days. The house was at one time the property of Harley Rodney Esq., who was a landowner of some repute in the area.

Nevill Hall has an interesting history. It was purchased by the Blaina Hospital Fund during the First World War. Prior to that, the Marquis of Abergavenny and one of the Vaughan families had owned it. Today, one of the largest hospitals in Wales covers the site of the park. The old hall still stands and is used as a conference centre.

The village of Llanfoist, looking towards Abergavenny, *c.* 1920. Abergavenny Cemetery is in the parish of Llanfoist; first opened in 1894, it is around 15 acres in size and serves the surrounding areas of the town. St Faith's church in Llanfoist is where former local MP Crawshay Bailey is buried. The church is perhaps best remembered for its Welsh-only services, which took place until around 1850.

Overleaf: The ruins of Llanhtony Priory can be found in the remote and beautiful Vale of Ewyas, which forms the valley of the Honddu river as it runs under the Black Mountains of Talgarth, west of the hilltop known as Mynydd Myrddin, or Merlin's Mount. It holds the remains of what was a priory of Austin Canons, founded between 1108 and 1136 by Hugh de Lacy, the Marcher Lord of Hereford. Prior to the present structure being built, there was a chapel on the site dedicated to St David of Wales. Walter de Gloucester, Constable of England, joined this community as a result of the amazing spiritual effect of the location. It was under Robert de Bethune, who succeeded Ernisius as prior, that the present structure was completed between 1180 and 1200. The strong influence of the priory resulted in a second Llanthony Abbey being established near Gloucester; the remains were later covered by railway sidings. The very remoteness of the location seems to have attracted men who wished to escape from the evils of the world but this same remoteness was its downfall. Gerald de Barri was known to have visited it in 1188 on his tour of Wales and he tells us how the first anchorites who settled there would not clear the woods or till the soil in case the place should lose its solitude and wildness. By the reign of Stephen, most of the monks no longer felt inclined to 'sing to the wolves' and many had moved to the abbey at Gloucester. Only a prior and four canons remained and the priory had no more than a shadowy existence until its dissolution under Henry VIII. Walter Savage Landor, the poet and friend of Browning and Swinburne, bought the priory, now known as Llanthony Abbey, in 1811. His early writings were done in Wales. However, Landor's grace in writing was not matched by his well-known temper and his attempt to revivify the priory failed largely because of his disputes with his neighbours. In 1814 he moved abroad.

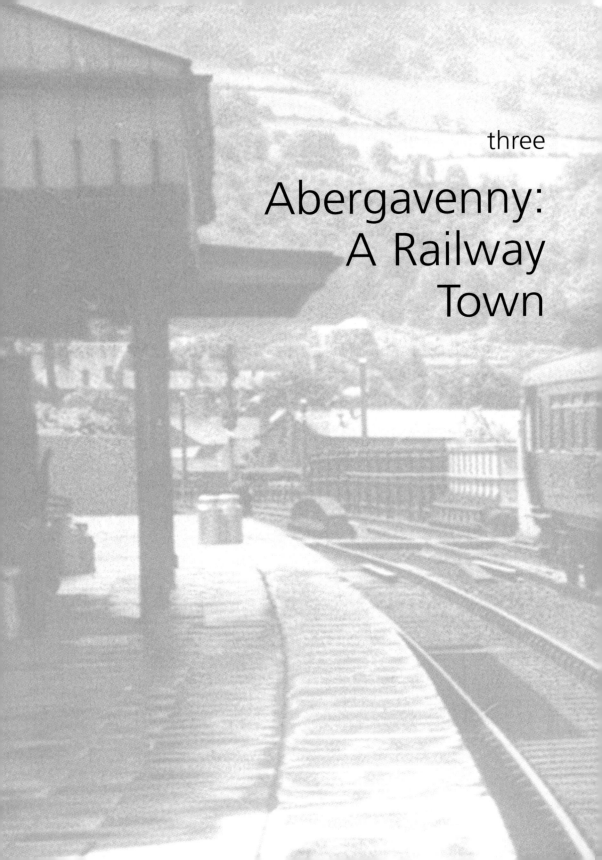

three

Abergavenny:
A Railway
Town

Like many towns in Great Britain, Abergavenny once had a good rail network and in some circles was known as the 'town amongst the mountains'. For the period of around 100 years it was considered to be one of the most important railway towns in South Wales. Between 1854 and 1958 there were three stations at Abergavenny. Sadly, there is just one station left, Monmouth Road, which provides a rail connection to Cardiff and Hereford. Little trace of the town's railway history can be found today in other parts of the town. The signal box, seen above in around 1975, stood on the Newport side of the station.

Abergavenny Monmouth Road railway station, *c.* 1960. The name Monmouth Road was used between 1950 and 1968. Today the station is just known as Abergavenny.

The railway once employed around 1,000 staff in the area and was at one time the town's biggest employer. Visitors to the Monmouth Road station today may be suprised to learn how large the station site once was. Still a very busy town for rail movements, in 1920 the sounds of the locomotives at work was known to echo around the hills overlooking the town and on a clear night the noise and volume of traffic was truly amazing.

A train from Hereford arriving at Llanfihangel station, *c.* 1950. Banking (assisting a train on a gradient) duties were required for many of the trains passing through. A locomotive banking a train from Abergavenny would drop away at this point.

Above and below: These two pictures show Abergavenny Monmouth Road station which, until the nationalisation of the railways in 1948, was a Great Western station. In the undated picture above we see a locomotive at work carrying out shunting duties. In the picture below, from around 1958, we see a view of the goods shed and cattle pens (to the right of the engines) and the still large amount of activity that the station complex commanded. Today, with just a minimal amount of staff required to carry out the station duties, it is surprising to learn that, around 1900, there were over forty employees at this location.

Webb coal tank No. 58888 arriving at the Junction in 1953. These coal tanks, remembered for their breathless exhaust sound, were lightly built but this belied their power output. Built between 1881 and 1897, they arrived in the area in around 1890. Built to haul freight, many were converted to haul passenger stock. Giving valiant service for over fifty years between Abergavenny, Merthyr and Tredegar, their wooden brake blocks were continuously applied on the steep descent from Brynmawr. This caused the axles to be forced against one side of the bearing by the pressure of the brake blocks on the wheels. This in turn caused the tyres to heat, resulting in loose tyres, fractured frames and frequent failures.

Webb coal tank No. 58926 at Abergavenny Junction, preparing to haul the last train to Merthyr on 5 January 1958.

A Great Western tank in the bay platform awaiting departure to Merthyr in 1957. Saturday 4 January 1958 was the last day of regular passenger service between Abergavenny and Merthyr. By that time, former Great Western pannier tanks from Merthyr shed often worked the passenger trains. Records indicate that the last down train, the 20.30 Abergavenny Junction to Merthyr, was hauled by GWR pannier tank No. 4630. The up train, working from Merthyr, was hauled by pannier tank No. 6423. Wagons from Govilon sidings were collected by Stanier 2-6-2 loco No. 40145.

The steam special, organised by the Midland area Stephenson Locomotive Society for the final run to Merthyr, at Abergavenny Monmouth Road, hauled by Super D No. 49121, on Sunday 5 January 1958. As a fitting tribute to the LNWR, the last train was hauled by two stalwart locomotives: Webb coal tank No. 58926 – already marked for preservation – and will soon join the train at Abergavenny Junction. The second locomotive, the Super D, had arrived from Tredegar shed. The coal tank's crew were driver G.E. Lewis and fireman Derek Hinton. The Super D crew was driver A.J. Brown and fireman A.E. Baker. The guard from Abergavenny was H. James.

A Webb coal tank arriving at Abergavenny Brecon Road from Brynmawr, tender first, c.1949. Moving in a south–westerly direction from Abergavenny Junction for 1¼ miles, Brecon Road was the next station. The bridge across Brecon Road can be seen in the background. Some of the station staff are standing on the platform on the right and there are milk churns on the opposite side.

A coal tank awaiting departure to Brynmawr in 1936. Brecon Road station had at one time a 5-ton crane. The station was very popular with passengers wishing to visit the town.

The locomotive steam shed just beyond Brecon Road station in 1938. The shed, which was close to the town's gasworks, had an allocation of nearly 100 engines. It consisted of four roads 290ft long, seven roads 162ft long and one road 133ft long, and could house forty-seven engines under cover. The pit road for dropping fires was found on the west side of the yard. This well-equipped shed also contained a very necessary wheel-drop. There was also a 50ft turntable, which operated from 1899 until 1953, and accommodation for railway crews was also found here. The importance of the shed can be judged by the fact that in LNWR days it was known by as shed No. 31 and had sub-sheds at Hereford (31H) Tredegar (31T) and Bleanavon. Engines allocated at the shed were more often than not used on the route to Merthyr; these were the Webb 0-6-2 coal tank, the 0-8-0 Super D and the infamous 0-8-4 tanks.

The railway and road bridge crossing the river Usk at Abergavenny. The railway bridge was built on columns in order to reduce the gradients on each side of the valley. The road bridge is at a lower level and is still in use toady. The railway bridge was removed during the early 1960s but it is still possible to find traces of it.

A freight train about to cross the railway bridge. Although the picture is of poor quality, the locomotive may be a 0-8-4 tank. These massive tanks were designed by H.P. Beames with the Welsh valleys in mind. The 0-8-4 tanks were seen on the line between 1923 and 1948. The engines caused many problems as it was soon apparent that, in certain places where curves were sharp, there was an almost full-time job for the permanent way men who were required to restore the straightened track to its proper shape after the engine had passed. This resulted in the Great Western Railway banning these engines on their metals.

Previous page: A passenger train to Merthyr crossing the River Usk in 1955. In early 1957 it was known in various circles that British Rail wanted to close the railway line between Abergavenny Junction and Merthyr. The line was one of the most expensive to work and closing the line would save British Rail £60,000 a year. The fact that freight was now negligible, and passenger traffic poor, meant that it was only a matter of time. The local weekly paper, the *Abergavenny Chronicle* ran a series of articles regarding the probable closure of the line. An article dated 10 May 1957 outlined the possible closure to the line, stating that careful consideration was being given. A possible solution to cost was mentioned in the form of the recently introduced diesel multiple units and simplified working methods. A railway magazine article on the line in 1957 stated it was not possible to use these trains due to limited clearance in the tunnels. While it was undoubtedly possible to find a solution to this problem, British Rail did not want to pay the costs involved.

Super D No. 4121 arriving at Abergavenny Junction. On Sunday 5 January 1958, when the last train left Abergavenny Junction at 12.45 p.m., the special with the coal tank leading ran towards the first stop at Govilon, hauling five eight-wheeler carriages. After a stop at Govilon, the long non-stop climb to Brynmawr continued; the load was not a difficult task for the two engines and their experienced crew. A water stop at Brynmawr was followed by a trip along the branch line to Ebbw Vale, which had closed to passengers in 1951.

four

Govilon

The last train from Abergavenny to Merthyr approaching the skew bridge between Llanfoist and Govilon on Sunday 5 January 1958. The Webb coal tank and the Super D are being worked in true LNWR style with the driver keeping the regulator full on. The line clings to the side of the Blorenge mountain as it coils itself onward and upward. A Red and White single-decker bus, one of the reasons for the closure of the railway, can be seen on the left. The return journey from Merthyr was made in the dark and by all accounts was a memorable journey for all concerned.

The train passes Govilon Wharf prior to arriving at Govilon station. Number 1 signal box, which dated from around 1911, was in this vicinity but is obscured by the building in this view.

The last train approaching the station at Govilon. It should be noted that the driver did not shut off steam until the train arrived at the platform edge and still the train stopped within the platform limits, due to the severe gradients on the line. The restart was spectacular and recorded on film.

Govilon station in London North Western days, *c.* 1905. The staff took great pride in performing their duties. The level crossing and No. 2 signal box can be seen in the background.

A Webb coal tank with three carriages arrives at Govilon station en route to Brynmawr in 1941. This view, looking east, shows the coal yard, to the left of the rail wagons, and signs of the war effort indicated by the white posts along the edge of the road to help drivers navigate during the blackout.

Station staff pose for the camera at Govilon station as closure of the line threatens in around 1957. The uniformed man on the left is stationmaster M. Bartlett. On the right is Mr Ralph Fulford, who was a signalman at Govilon for around fifty years. The booking office window can be seen on the left.

More passengers seem to be using Govilon station as closure threatened. around 1957, perhaps because, unlike the stations of Gilwern and Clydach, Govilon station was near to the village. The couple walking towards the camera have been identified as Mr and Mrs Harris of Cwm Lane.

The post office in Govilon, with the name of J.Davies, grocer, standing proudly above the door. The lack of road transport in the picture signifies that the best form of transport at the time was the railway. As road traffic increased after the Second World War, the village often became congested as large vehicles, especially double-decker buses and lorries, tried to negotiate their way through the village. No doubt it was a relief to many of the locals when the Heads of the Valleys road opened in the early sixties, which meant that traffic bypassed the village.

Opposite above: The drawbridge at Govilon, approximately half a mile away from the village. This bridge over the Brecknock and Abergavenny Canal gives access to Llanwwenarth House. The canal was built between 1797 and 1800 and at one time provided a highly effective form of transport for local goods.

Opposite below: A view over Govilon from Blorenge mountain in 1978.

Post Office, Govilon.

A later view of the post office at Govilon. The telephone service has arrived and there are signs on the post office wall and on the telegraph pole opposite advertising the public telephone. The road towards Gilwern curves to the right of the picture and the blacksmith can be seen dealing with a customer in the background. At that time, the local blacksmith provided one of the most important services in the village and his services would be required by many that owned horses and ponies. This would include such people as the doctor, vicar and undertaker. The value of a horse was such that proper shoeing was so important that the horse owner would choose a blacksmith with great care. The type of shoe used depended on such factors as the breed of horse, the type of work it did and the way it habitually handled its feet.

Village, Govilon.

Govilon village, with the blacksmith's shop on the right beyond the bushes. On the left is the church hall; Govilon church stood opposite but is out of shot. The three houses on the ridge were canal properties. By the 1960s, this road was carrying a large volume of local traffic and the single- and double-decker buses of the Red and White Bus Co. regularly passed through. One Saturday afternoon, a double-decker bus en route to Abergavenny crashed into the post office as it travelled round the corner pictured here. One of the injured passengers was local man Mr David Turner from Gilwern.

Above Govilon village is the Blorenge mountain, which stands at a height of 1,834ft. The road up to Blaenavon gives an excellent view of the outstanding countryside on a fine day. The same, however, cannot be said on a cold winter's day, when mist can engulf the mountain and road, making driving conditions extremely hazardous. As the road approaches Govilon on the steep descent, motorists have to drive around the notorious Fiddler's Elbow. Many road accidents have occurred on this road, often resulting in fatalities, and this has given rise to stories of phantom motorists and pedestrians. Despite this, numerous places to park can be found along the road, making it a popular visitor attraction.

The top of the Blorenge, close to the Keeper's Pond above the town of Blaenavon, is another popular tourist attraction and again is ideal on summer days for afternoon picnics. The pond is used for a variety of purposes, including fishing and model boating. The town of Blaenavon is located on a lofty hillside around a mile away. Suffering regularly from inclement weather, it is not unusual for the town to be cut off for short periods after a heavy snowfall. Buried close by the pond is Foxhunter, the famous showjumping horse belonging to Sir Harry Llewelyn.

The industrial and mining town of Blaenavon can today boast many tourist attractions, reminding and informing visitors of the past. These include an ironworks founded in around 1788, although iron ore smelting dates in this area from the sixteenth century. By the time the works closed in 1900, it had become the largest in the area. Arguably now the major attraction of the town is Big Pit, which closed in 1980 after 100 years in existence. The working men's institute situated in Lion Street dates from 1883 and is well worth viewing. Blaenavon once boasted two railway stations: one owned by the Great Western Railway and closed to passenger service in 1962, the other the former London and North Western station. This station complex included a goods shed and engine shed; it closed to passengers in May 1941, the engine shed closing in 1934. Little trace of the Great Western Railway can now be found, although the Pontypool and Blaenavon Railway is flourishing as a tourist attraction.

five

Water in
The Valley

Ferry, Govilon

Otter hunting on the River Usk at Gilwern

River Usk, Gilwern

The River Usk at Gilwern, *c.* 1910. Otters tend to live in dens near to or by the side of water, often with an underwater entrance. They feed on small fish, birds and frogs. They give birth to litters of around five pups, the young remaining with the mother for a period of one year. Often hunted for their furs, it is probable that the river was extinct of the breed by 1970. However, a campaign to restore otters to their natural habitat will hopefully lead to the breed being seen in the Usk once more. Pollution of the river at this time was not a problem.

Opposite above: The Govilon ferry, *c.* 1938. The ferry once operated on the River Usk and the wooden boat and the wires across the river, which were used during the ferry's operation, are clearly visible. Ferries like this have provided conveyance for passengers and goods across a river or other body of water for hundreds of years. It is many years since this ferry operated and is forgotten by many, while others may be surprised to learn that a ferry ever existed.

Opposite below: Otter hunting on the River Usk at Gilwern, *c.* 1910. The otter hound has been in the country since the twelfth century and this form of hunting was very popular during the nineteenth century. The dog's coarse and oily coat helped the dog to withstand the water. Webbed feet also made the animal adept at swimming.

Ty Mawr Fire. 19.3.06 F. Temple

No doubt the fire brigade were grateful for the close proximity of the River Usk when called to deal with this fire, which occurred at Ty Mawr House on 19 March 1906. The first fire engines appeared in the seventeenth century and were simply tubs carried on runners, long poles or wheels; water was still supplied to the fire site by a bucket brigade. The invention of a hand-stitched leather hosepipe in the Netherlands in around 1672 enabled firefighters to work closer to the fire without endangering their engines and increased the accuracy of the water placement. At about the same time, the development of pumping devices made it possible to draw water from rivers and ponds. A cotton-covered rubber hose was developed in around 1870. The steam-pump fire engine, introduced in London in 1829 by John Ericsson and John Braithwaite, was used in many large cities by the 1850s. Some were self-propelled but most used horses for propulsion, conserving steam pressure for the pump.

Opposite above: A family out for a walk by the canal while the man on the bridge surveys the peaceful scene. More in formation on the Brecknock and Abergavenny Canal can be found in *Around Gilwern*. The canal, which meanders along towards Brecon, is still a tranquil place.

Opposite below: Clydach Waterfalls. The Clydach Valley is renowned for its series of wooded nooks and picturesque waterfalls, which provide breathtaking views. The waterfalls falling into the pools below make a very worthwhile visit. The raging torrent, which the River Clydach can soon become, is perhaps viewed from a safe distance but on a fine summer's day the climb down to the pools below over the often slippery rocks is extremely rewarding. The beauty of the River Clydach and its waterfalls is unseen by many of the visitors to the area.

Clydach Waterfall near Brynmawr

Above: A spectacular view of one of the many waterfalls found on the River Clydach. William Shakespeare (1564–1616) is rumoured to have written *A Midsummer Night's Dream* in a cave in the Clydach Gorge in around 1595. The play is thought by many to be outstanding among his comedies. It interweaves several plots involving two pairs of noble lovers, a group of bumbling and unconsciously comic townspeople and members of the fairy realm, notably Puck, King Oberon and Queen Titania. We can never be certain if the legend that he wrote *A Midsummer Night's Dream* here is true but it certainly enhances the awesome beauty and reputation of the river Clydach.

Left: Clydach Lower Falls. Waterfalls can develop in several ways; different rates of erosion where a resistant layer of rock in a streambed overlies softer layers is the principal manner. As time goes by, subsequent erosion of the softer rock by the falling water undermines and periodically breaks off portions of harder rock. In mountainous regions, waterfalls generally develop where a glacier has deepened a major trunk valley, leaving less eroded branch valleys hanging. Thus the tributary streams in these valleys discharge into the main river.

This is Pwll-Ress Falls, Gilwern, on the River Clydach, *c.* 1910. The bridge was popular among local inhabitants at one time for Sunday afternoon walks and may hold many memories for the older generation.

CLYDACH FALLS, ABERGAVENNY

Clydach Valley, Brynmawr.

Pont Harry Isaac, near Brynmawr, *c.* 1900. The population of Gilwern, Clydach and Brynmawr is now considerably larger than when the postcard was produced. While there have been many redevelopments in the area, the natural beauty has remained.

Opposite above: The River Clydach, as it gains momentum rushing down the gorge. This breathtaking picture may make readers feel as if they are standing on the banks of the river.

Opposite below: The Clydach Valley as it once looked. Improvements are continual and the Heads of the Valley Road was many years away. With the passing of time, the older generation who remember this scene pass on and we must be thankful for pictures like this to keep the memories alive.

Brynmawr. Brec. Showing Tramroad

The start of the Old Black Rock Road, as it leaves Brynmawr, can be seen on the left. To the right is the route that the Heads of the Valleys Road took when it was built in the early 1960s. The date of the picture is not known.

Opposite above: Clydach Bridge, Brynwawr. This postcard was produced in around 1920 by S. Davies & Son, printers and stationers in Brynmawr.

Opposite below: A view of Brynmawr, with the river Clydach on the left, *c.* 1910. Published by G. Bowen of Brynmawr, the picture was phototyped in Berlin.

CLYDACH BRIDGE, BRYNMAWR

Brynmawr.

The unique Clydach Gorge in all its splendid beauty, *c.* 1985.

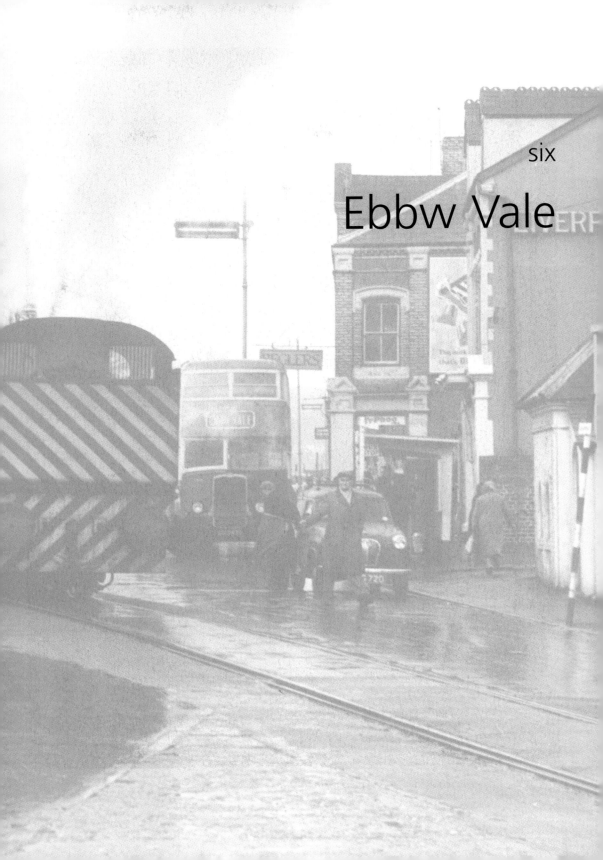

six

Ebbw Vale

View of Ebbw Vale (from Mynydd-Manmoel Mountain)

The town of Ebbw Vale lies in a valley about 17 miles from Newport and straddles the waves of steep little hills that surround the valley. Ebbw Vale ranks as an urban district and, as with so many coalfield communities, the impetus of industrialism in the nineteenth century made it not so much a centre of communal life but an area where workers and their families were closely grouped together. For many years, the townspeople depended on coal for its survival. As with many towns in the South Wales valleys, as the decline of that industry began there was a drop in the population of 12 per cent between 1939 and 1946. By this time, a huge steelworks had spread, providing new industry to the area and becoming the dominant feature of the town. Ebbw Vale thus became an important steel town that fitted well into Great Britain's steel industry.

In the 1950s, the population of Ebbw Vale dropped by 10 per cent to just over 29,000. This was better than other towns in the area, such as Abertillery and Tredegar, who both recorded a fall of 12 per cent. Tredegar stands between Ebbw Vale and Merthyr Tydfil, in an area that at one time had much the same interest in coal but lost to Ebbw Vale its once considerable steel industry.

Market Street, Ebbw Vale. Perhaps one of the most famous people associated with Ebbw Vale was Aneurin (Nye) Bevan (1897-1960), who was the Labour MP for Ebbw Vale. His posts included Minister of Health from 1945-51, and later Minister of Labour and National Service. He was married to Jennie Lee. Aneurin Bevan launched the National Health Service, which it is believed to have been based on Tredegar's Workmen's Medical Aid Association.

The Ebbw Vale steelworks once employed thousands of men and was in fact one of the region's largest employers. As in the coal mining industry, son followed father and grandfather into the steelworks. The local schools such as Brynmawr, Tredegar and Ebbw Vale encouraged boys entering their final school year to seek apprenticeships at the Ebbw Vale steelworks. Many believed that by gaining employment at the steelworks they had a secure job for life. Today, most of the site has been knocked down for redevelopment and the industry is quietly being forgotten.

Opposite above: The blast furnaces of the steelworks. The manufacture of iron and steel, and the technology used in the production of iron and its alloys, is a particularly interesting subject. The differences between the various types of iron and steel are sometimes confusing because of the nomenclature used. Steel in general is an alloy of iron and carbon, often with an admixture of other elements. Some alloys that are commercially called irons contain more carbon than commercial steels. Open-hearth iron and wrought iron contain only a few hundredths of 1 per cent of carbon. Steels of various types contain from 0.04 per cent to 2.25 per cent of carbon. Cast iron, malleable cast iron and pig iron contain amounts of carbon varying from 2 to 4 per cent. A special form of malleable iron, containing virtually no carbon, is known as white-heart malleable iron. A special group of iron alloys, known as ferroalloys, is used in the manufacture of iron and steel alloys; they contain from 20 to 80 per cent of an alloying element, such as manganese, silicon or chromium.

Opposite below: A view of the works known locally as Victoria Furnaces. Modern steel manufacture employs blast furnaces that are in fact simply refinements of the furnaces used by the old ironworkers. The process of refining molten iron with blasts of air was accomplished by the British inventor Sir Henry Bessemer, who developed the Bessemer furnace, or converter, in 1855. Since the 1960s, several so-called mini mills have been producing steel from scrap metal in electric furnaces. The giant steel mills remain essential for the production of steel from iron ore.

Victoria Furnaces Ebbw Vale 608

The running off of slag from a blast furnace. Another well-known MP was Michael Foot, who was Deputy Leader of the Labour Party from 1979-80 and then Leader from 1980-83. He was MP for Ebbw Vale from 1960-83 and Blaenau Gwent from 1983-92. He had also been Lord President of the Council, Secretary of State for Employment from 1974-76 and Leader of the House of Commons from 1976-79. He was the Labour MP for Devonport in 1945-55. He was Aneurin Bevan's biographer and was married to Jill Craigie. Foot's efforts in attempting to keep the steelworks open for as long as possible was highly regarded by many of his constituents.

Opposite above: Two of the many thousands of men who worked at the steelworks. Clearly proud of their industry, they convey memories of a steel industry long ago. The exact date at which people discovered the technique of smelting iron ore to produce usable metal is not known. The earliest iron implements discovered by archaeologists in Egypt date from about 3000 BC and iron ornaments were used even earlier; the comparatively advanced technique of hardening iron weapons by heat treatment was known to the Greeks in around 1000 BC.

Opposite below: Part of the once-huge steelworks complex. The alloys produced by early ironworkers, and indeed all the iron alloys made until around the fourteenth century, would be classified today as wrought iron. They were made by heating a mass of iron ore and charcoal in a forge or furnace having a forced draft. Under this treatment, the ore was reduced to the sponge of metallic iron filled with a slag composed of metallic impurities and charcoal ash. This sponge of iron was removed from the furnace while still incandescent and beaten with heavy sledges to drive out the slag and to weld and consolidate the iron.

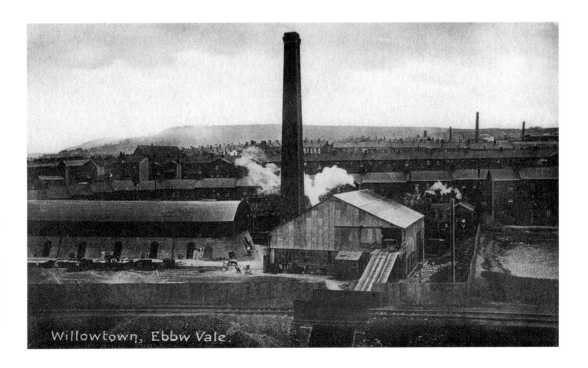

Willowtown, Ebbw Vale.

A locomotive en route to the steelworks, *c.* 1959. It is leaving the by now closed LNWR station behind. In 1961 the steelworks had an allocation of around forty conventional steam engines, together with two steam Sentinels and four diesel locomotives. The extensive rail

network around the site signifies the size and importance of the works. At that time, a visitor to the works was likely to meet fitters who were able to give information regarding the entire history of each engine the company owned.

A view of Ebbw Vale and the steelworks in winter, *c.* 1930. Snow could cause severe problems for everyone in the area and heavy snowfalls were not uncommon at the time. Although the snow has covered the area, hiding the bleak landscape, it is possible to see just how deep the snow could be. It is possible to imagine a steelworker having to dig his way out of his house in order to walk to work on a cold bleak morning.

Opposite above: A panoramic view of the steelworks at Ebbw Vale, showing just some of the vast site complex. In the foreground, it is possible to see the large number of railway wagons required to help run the works. To the left are some of the many houses needed to accommodate the families of the workers.

Opposite below: The original steelworks, which dated back to 1790, closed in 1929. Richard Thomas & Co. built a completely new and modern steel strip plant in 1935. Steel manufacture ended at the works in 1973, although tin plate manufacture continued for some considerable time after that date. The main office, complete with clock tower, can be seen on the left. During the Second World War, Lord Haw Haw commented that the clock was five minutes fast, which it was, and this sent shivers down the backs of local residents. All the buildings on the right have now been demolished.

Overleaf: Ebbw Vale Low Level station, *c.* 1959. Ebbw Vale once boasted two railway stations. This was the former Great Western station; passenger services ended on 30 April 1962. From 1958 onwards, the steam engines were often replaced by diesel multiple units in an effort to cut costs and improve the service. Sadly, by June 1961 proposals had been made for the withdrawal of the passenger service.

Ebbw Vale Low Level station, when it was under the control of the Great Western Railway. The famous Eugene Cross Park, home of Ebbw Vale Rugby Football Club, lies behind the station buildings. Like many rugby clubs in South Wales, famous internationals have played for the team. This includes Arthur Smith, who played for Scotland between 1954 and 1962. Captain of his country on fifteen occasions, he also led the British Lions on their tour of South Africa in 1962. Arthur Lewis gained eleven caps for Wales between 1969 and 1973 and was captain on three occasions. Clive Burgess scored a try on his debut for Wales in 1976 and represented his country on six occasions.

Another view of Ebbw Vale Low Level station, again in its Great Western days, *c.* 1910. This picture was taken from a higher level and gives a better view of the station site. The single platform and station building are clearly visible.

Ebbw Vale Low Level station on 27 July 1957. A number of passengers can be seen on the platform, signifying that at that time the station was well patronised. Sadly, as the next decade drew closer, the availability of the motor car to many signalled the death knell of this and many other branch lines.

Ebbw Vale High Level station, a London North Western station. This photograph gives an insight into the size of the station complex. At one time there was a signal box at this location, built in 1890. Having closed on 10 January 1952, the signal box was removed long before the rest of the site. Complete redevelopment of the area has now taken place.

Ebbw Vale High Level station in July 1959, with the station complex nearly deserted. The station was known as High Level from 23 May 1949. The final timetable made interesting reading, with only two departures shown. However, on Saturdays five extra departures were shown. No trains ran on Sunday. James Street was located to the right of the picture.

The last train before the closure of the line, pictured just after its arrival at Ebbw Vale High Level station on 5 January 1958. The branch line from Beaufort had closed to passenger traffic on 2 April 1951. However, the freight service continued until 2 November 1959.

Passengers exploring the station complex after the arrival of the last train in January 1958. This shows just how many people travelled on the last train. This was not the first passenger special to visit, as a two-coach special had previously visited in 1953. No trace of the station can now be found and people trying to establish where the station once stood can only use the church in the background as a guideline.

The Station. Beaufort. 571

The Station. Beaufort

This view of Beaufort station, again from around 1920, also shows part of the town. The town has been in existence since the latter part of the 1700s, springing up as a result of the coming of the ironworks.

Opposite above: The junction for the line to Ebbw Vale in July 1959, after the Abergavenny to Merthyr line had closed. The signal box housed the single-line equipment for the branch, which opened in March 1914. Beaufort Viaduct was close by but, like the railway, all traces of it have been removed.

Opposite below: Beaufort station, *c.* 1920. Some shunting movements are taking place in the distance. The town had a recorded population of around 3,000 at the turn of the century and this doubled during the next sixty years. The town was 1,200ft above sea level and was often cut off during the severe winters that once gripped the country. Beaufort station was no exception and was known to be cut off on more than one occasion.

Beaufort station on 16 July 1959, after the closure of the Abergavenny to Merthyr line. The air of abandonment and decay are evident. During the 1960s the station complex was completely filled in and the area has now been redeveloped. It is not possible to find any trace of the station site.

Opposite above: Rassau, a small village close to Beaufort and Ebbw Vale, *c.* 1920. The community was originally formed by sheep farmers. The closeness of some of the cottages and the tight curves of the tramway perhaps signify the closeness of the people and community at that time. The area has now been redeveloped and the picture serves as a memory to remind us of the quarries in the area, which the tramway once served.

Opposite below: The Arch, Ebbw Vale, a reminder of the history and architecture of the town. Since the end of the Second World War, a large amount of redevelopment has taken place around the town of Ebbw Vale. The steel industry which made the town famous is no more, the mines of the area a distant memory. The people of the town have had to adjust, seeking alternative employment and learn new skills. They have adapted and moved on and they are proud of the way of life that once was.

Rassau, Beaufort.

T. Harding Son & Co's
Bristol
Real Photo Series.

The Great Western Railway station at Cwm, *c*. 1925. The station served the community well until the closure of the passenger service in 1962. The railway continued to serve the steelworks and local collieries for many years afterwards. Now, with both industries no longer in existence, there are plans

to reopen the line to a passenger service once again. Perhaps in the not-too-distant future, Cwm will again have a railway station and the sound of passengers talking awaiting the arrival of a train will once again be heard.

Other local titles published by Tempus

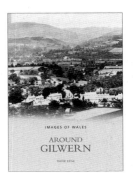

Around Gilwern

DAVID EDGE

The view of the Clydach Gorge is arguably one of the most spectacular in South Wales today. Until the closure of the Abergavenny to Merthyr Railway in 1958, passengers travelling the line were able to see for themselves the magnificent and sometimes brutal scenery of the area. *Around Gilwern* illustrates how the area has changed in recent years and will appeal to all those who previously knew the area and inform the casual visitor of the rich history this region has to offer.

0 7524 3285 0

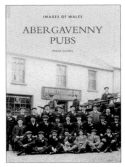

Abergavenny Pubs

FRANK OLDING

Using images held in the archives of the Abergavenny Museum this illustrated volume of the town's pubs traces the development of the licensed trade in this fascinating area of Wales. *Abergavenny Pubs* will delight all those who want to know more about the history of the town's pubs, their clientele, landlords and ladies and take the reader on a fascinating journey into the past of their favourite local.

0 7524 3576 0

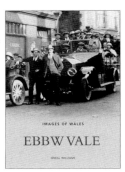

Ebbw Vale

IDWAL WILLIAMS

Ebbw Vale's strong industrial history is well represented in this comprehensive collection of nearly 200 archive images, some of which date from as early as the 1900s. This book recalls life as it once was before the huge loss of steel industry jobs, and depicts the history of this part of Gwent in terms of its society, its culture and its industry. With pictures as varied as Rassau Road street scenes and miners's strikes, this book is a fast-moving glimpse of this area's bustling history.

0 7524 3209 5

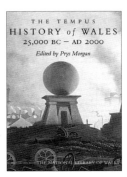

The Tempus History of Wales

PRYS MORGAN

Wales was at the heart of the Industrial Revolution, with towns like Merthyr Tydfil driving the engine of the British Empire. The cultural and social divide between modern, industrialised Wales and the traditional agricultural areas is explored within this comprehensive volume.

0 7524 1983 8

If you are interested in purchasing other books published by Tempus, or in case you have difficulty finding any Tempus books in your local bookshop, you can also place orders directly through our website

www.tempus-publishing.com